Batmanticism

Poems by

Chad Parmenter

in case of emergency press

We are proud to acknowledge the Traditional Owners of country throughout Australia and to recognise their continuing connection to land, waters, and culture.

We pay our respects to their Elders past, present, and emerging.

We support recognition, reconciliation, and reparation.

in case of emergency press

http://www.icoe.com.au

Batmanticism

Poems

Chad Parmenter

Published by In Case of Emergency Press 2021

Copyright 2021 © Chad Parmenter

All rights reserved. Without limiting the rights under copyright reserved above, no part of this publication may be reproduced, stored in or introduced into a database and retrieval system or transmitted in any form or any means (electronic, mechanical, photocopying, recording or otherwise) without the prior written permission of the owner of copyright.

Cover and Title Page photo by Mark Asthoff, photo of bat by Husen Siraaj

Photo of the Author by Anastasia Pottinger

ISBN 978-0-6451280-3-1

Table of contents

"I AM BATMAN"	**1**
The Batcave	3
Notes for a Comic Book Artist to See By	5
Opening Night	8
Batman In Honey	11
Is Batman Trapped in the Past?	13
Osiris	16
Batplaning Over the Rainbow	20
In Mr. Freeze's Glacierworks	23
Our Hero *Is* Trapped in the Past!	25
The Bat-Can-Can	27
In Honey B	30
Closing Time	33
His Valediction Forbidding Becoming Like Him	36
Batellite, Batellite of Love	37
Batman Agonistes, or Eyeless in Gotham	40
BAT & MAN	**43**
Hey, Bruce. Wake up. You're shrieking in your sleep.	45
You dreamed your parents made you by the bay?	46
So bats conceived you, just as much as Tom?	47
What did you dream then, sobbing in a ball?	48
You murmured for your soldiers and your war.	49
You said you made the dark a kinder god.	50
Did heroes guard you through the darkest part?	51
You fought your parents just before they died.	52
and think of Arkham. Nightmares took you there?	53
What heroes nursed you in the orphanage?	54
You loved the part where partying was life.	55
What made you say the underworld has come?	56

Go on.	57
This really happened. I remember. You went underground.	58
Some nightmare fire erupted from your wounds?	59
and now. Some dream—sounds Batmanic to me.	60
Batman Leaves a Sonnet On Catwoman's Voicemail	61
ACKNOWLEDGEMENTS	63
ABOUT THE AUTHOR	65

Batmanticism

*Okay. A kid, I prayed, but to the world
to stay away. To me, alone felt whole
and, holy solipsist, my eyes slid closed,
and then the sense of eyelessness began
with I-lessness not far behind. Unseen
because the dream of seeing disappeared,
I turned unreal. The old reality
would merge with my old self outside a mind
that knew it was the only thing alive,
a cave, and I its god. The world appeared
to end my prayer, but as a shattered mirror
I couldn't see me in.*

    from "Batman Agonistes, or Eyeless in Gotham"

Many friends, family and loved ones have helped make this book possible, and I'm grateful. And to poets whose work served as inspiration and example—especially Bryan Dietrich, Allison Joseph, Kevin Young, and Stephanie Burt—thank you.

"I am Batman"

Bob Kane, creator of Batman

The Batcave

> *Only the most successful heroes… had a secret lair.*
> —Michael Chabon

It's his living grave.

Here, every morning,
he kind of, like, dies.

The supercomputers mutter-purr
his elegies; the cobalt vaults chant out bats.

After a bad impression of rest,
he's gassing the batplane.

Something in us wants to write our lines
into his thought balloons:
"I stop. I sleep. I grieve."
But what kind of machine would he be then?

Now the batphone glows rose, another end
of the world he'd better end.

And the racked batsuits will wait for him.
And the dark arsenal, and the carnival of criminal
tricks, will guard themselves well enough.
And the museum will hold its plastirama dinosaur,
its penny too heavy for even God—and by that
I mean Dad—to hold, its infinite, scintillant
kinds of armor, far from any
visitors but us.

The plugged miles of tunnels will keep
leading to hell,
and we will pray that they will stay
sealed.

The batplane cockpit locks him in.
Its turbines purr like our best pets
used to.

Batman, maybe we don't need to be
buried in work, in worry,
anymore.

We ink your thinking to yourself,
"What a wonderful
underworld," but have you ever
seen the world above evil?

This lair, hard as dark
to part with,
we may one day flood
with light.

Just not tonight.

Notes for a Comic Book Artist to See By

Make it Christmas, so the holes of white light
in the blank, black sky hold the haloes
of each erasure of a star.

Commissioner Gordon handing Batman a red
box in a green bow.

Batman: SORRY, JIM, THE ONLY GIFT
               I CAN TAKE IS PAIN.

Closeup on the Arkham Asylum sign.

Gordon freeing Hugo Strange (Golden Age
maker of monsters), light like ice on his spectacles.

The monster: Wintergeist. Use your own powers
of visualization. Like Iceland hybridized with
a chandelier, fragile enough to be shattered by light,
it can't hurt anything.

This is the gift you'll write into Batman's hands:
a weapon to hit from far away; let it spit a signifier
of fire.
Sound effects: SHUSH SHUSH SHUSH
Make them that dark-light alternation—white
like snow seen on tv. That bright.

End with a downtown Christmas vista

oranged over with the color of destruction.

    Here's the story that ghosts
    the batfantasia, if it will help you
    make the lines dark and thick:

    I'm seven years younger.
    Masks of snow thicken the soles of my shoes.

    The wander behind my girlfriend turns her
    from indigo figurehead
    to blue rune.

    I focus on her, let our cohered tunnel
    vision white out the art building
    I used to belong to,

    and in combat boots
    she's snowshoeing past its missing windows
    to me, and I think I must have been thinking

    who better to live with me in the
    SHANTIH SHANTIH SHANTIH dead
    peace of the end of *The Wasteland*,

    where there were no heroes except fears,
    because her living room glows with tv snow,
    and her breath froths out

    in soft monsters
    that a wave of a glove
    tears open.

See—Wintergeist as Christmas past:
a tracery of gray steam, splintering into silver air.

When Batman finishes him off,
don't let his mouth round up into a grin;
leave it as the slash that shows
you jabbed your pen using something
that hurt you to remember, too.

        Then inhale. Now let it go.

Opening Night

It begins with an iridescent hiss
in his police radio:

> "Joker has broken
> into the Sacred Heart
> Shelter. Madman,
>
> he planted bulbs
> that grow too fast
> in the midnight snacks.

Some kind of rose called Opening Night.
Grows thorns in those homeless throats."

His mask fits like a bad kiss—
too tight. Just right.

> So do the blue gloves.
> They draw his fingers
> into the bony
> beginnings of wings.
>
> Like anything
> being born,
> he knows no choice,
> only "go."

The Batcave, good womb, lets him.
The Batmobile, bad cradle,

> rattles as it delivers him
> to a city red with need.

He sees the sirens fireplate the skyline.
He sees the bats flash, a tide of black ink,
above the bay, in its moon-blue suit.

I think he hears their wings
whispering things like,
"To be created is to be erased,"
like a bedtime story below the roar
of a nightmare, and I swear

they hammer a murmur of answer
to the flutter and smother of his one, held breath.

Night hides him in its cool cover art. Then parts,

and the arteries and interstates
of the outskirts glitter him in.

Here's the city center,
colonized by constellations

> of street lights whose battery
> hearts need to be recharged.

> Listen: if you're wearing
> my same face, erased by change,

if you stay in a shelter made of one, old story,
with no new emotions to go home to,

tell your own persona the one-syllable hymn
Gotham acts in phantom pantomime,

with its needle-steepled cathedrals,
with its gargoyles crying rain,

with its red tide
of sirens writing

        blood lightning
        on Batman's mask.

        Tell it *help*.

Batman In Honey

—meaning love. Meet Julie Moneybunch,
    needy as a cathedral, oh yes, rose window

broken open, darkness in her narthex. She's nixed
    the waggle-dances of gangsters, been repaid

in spades by their noir icons: poison host,
    bap-bap-baptism by tommy gun. Second one

seeded her armorless heart with bullets. Holy
    Fertility, Batman, if the spent shells didn't evolve

to bumblebees, tumble free of the street
    to sting the hitmen. Julie wasn't even hurt. Ever

have such Hollywood miracles flowered here,
    on the pop top of hoodoo. Who wouldn't be

unsuited by her plea: *Ditch the wings. Drink me
    honey.* Especially remembering Joker's leggy cyborg,

the river of silver wire she cried toward his eyes,
    her gray lasers set on Braise. Not much better,

that summer in Poison Ivy's winding lies,
    green hands planting an itch deeper than feeling,

turning our hero to pillar of blisters. Lost lovers
    clutter his cave, molding shadows to hollow statues.

True, he's hottest for you, Gotham. Lines he writes,
    Christ—*Rain is her hair. Neon a fringe in her lingerie*

bridges. In your batblack alleys, he waits to cage
    the same dream that honeycombs puppy love—fantasy

as distance, drained of ways to render heroes drones.
    But his hive is night. He's already inside. So Julie

will stay sweet. Then leave. Poor drone. This one will sting.

Is Batman Trapped in the Past?

Sweetheart
of the moment,

does he police
your meter heart,

steering it into
the hot zone,

but leaving
his blue gloves on?

While you two
suit up new love,

does he cave
into old ones?

What he loved:
the tv series.

Julie Newmar wore
Lurex, whiskers

of perfect silk, purred
until he entered

her chain-link
catacombs.

Leopard-printed
cronies tore in.

ZOK, WOK,
POW—shrouds

on the screen,
such bat-tastic shades

on pain. Maybe
he searches your nerves

for these. At least,
he fantasizes you

into Episode Number
Whatever, "The

Catwoman Goeth."
In the Morpheus

Mattress Factory,
your cat's cradle

knots him to the belt
rolling slowly under

the Button Puncher.
Factory of tragedy,

it traps him still.

So, for now,

forgive his drift
in the silver hiss

of her abyss.
Forgive him reading,

in the air above you,
the red word

your needle would
spell as it fell.

Osiris

Oh yes, it is everyone's favorite
god of the dead, matte-blue as the bat suit
once was, cut like Skeletor before
that steroid scandal stormed
Castle Greyskull,
eyes ice, mind mad, ride rad,

but he doesn't roll, no, he tsunamis
into Gotham on a monsoon
of scarabs, his entourage posh—
        undead headliners
like Pac, like the last crush you left,

and shouldn't have. He takes
the stage. That is to say, he makes
his own: the skyline his headlight
        eyes turn pyrite.
The smog tries to mummy him up,

but he pollutes the pollution.
Imagine what he does then. I can't.

If I have to... death happens. Then
more. Ink in gore.

Batman, batapult through the roof
of the C-Note Casino.
Osiris is colliding with its major players.

He does this uncool thing:
gleams a deep, sea-on-Venus amethyst,
and it burns through human skin
like a curse, like birth
reversed, it player-hates their
spirits away like Pat Boone
used to.

They rise as ka's, brittle, shriveled souls,
and they whisper like pages of scripture
coming apart, like papyrus on papyrus
flitting out of this tight night.

I know you don't know what to do.
I write an adze into your hand,
and say you have no soul for him to kill.

Go: dice this Osiris, like Diddy did
"Kashmir", but with these comic book
sound effects, deader than Eliot's:

    SKAK   SKUKK   SLISH

You do. You kill. Guilt is all he leaves
with you. This has to be past finished.
But this is the myth Osiris lives:

> That Set dismembers him,
> and Isis turns bling-bright
> with deep grief, and its tragic
> magic gives her this trick:
> stitching him back to life.

So she careens in, her needle gold bone,
her thread of some pimp sinew hissing
as it lashes him back to himself.

Bats, you have no anchor here;
you can't not sink. But flash that adze
again and again, and again, she'll
enfranchise her Frankenstein back to life,
back to the battle you need him to be,
and by "you",
I mean "I".

But we can't not try.
Quote some Auden at him.
"Poetry makes nothing happen."
What a fun thought, but nothing
but nothing makes nothing happen.
I buried some Berryman badly
in the last stanza.
Maybe he'll zombie on down there
and eat that spotlight vampire's mind.

But you go it alone, don't you?
And none of these poets
wrote what your blank look
shows me you need:

> a simple, dumb
> hymn to the sun.
> Remember now, how
> it never left.

      And, chanting it, feel real
      heat. You do. I do, too.

And in this abyss
that was the high
rollers' paradise,
watch that hot light

march, bleach away
the meat market
of bodies he made
lay still. It kills him
because we can't.
We're not written to.

Now go home. Then rest.
Then rise. Then shine.

Batplaning Over the Rainbow

Darling, Carl Jung said we all need
a rainbow to be chained to, i.e.

an infinity we couldn't reach
to keep ourselves here, or heroes.

What could stay more safely away
than the past? So it prisms my sky.

        I.e.
        my dream:

Batman ropes a perfect, lurex batarang
around a rainbow. It holds him,

then lets him go. He falls, dissolves
like a black lifesaver under your tongue.

The rainbow falls by its own weight.
Flames crusade in its invisible stitches.

        You croon
        Batman

awake in your living room. Cloudbursts
powered its wet gloom. Curtains

filter it silver. The water in his hero stare
makes it a rainbow. But the batplane pants

on your roof. It will zoom him home
through the monochrome sky.

>   But a, what,
>   murder?

of rainbows waits there, first curled
into circles, then melting to echo

the letting go of our summer together.
He tailspins in. Mist paints his wingtips.

Let him land in the bed-sized hand
of Carl Jung, whose tongue clunks,

>   *Come*
>   *home.*

His hangar lungs ring like the batphone.
Superhero of lucid dreamers, Jung

shakes Batman half-awake. I say not yet.
Take off that rainbow halo. Follow

with your imaginary whiskers. Begin
to strip the mask of ink. Don't go

>   fast; don't turn
>   to rain.

When you do, too soon,
I'll hear my own pulse

as the chink of a clock in tin.
I'll live with Batman's safe, paper heart;

he'll try out the silence in

        mine.
        Bye.

In Mr. Freeze's Glacierworks

From the time of his first appearance in 1958 onward, Mr. Freeze was portrayed as one of the many "joke" villains (see also Killer Moth), cast as stock enemies of Batman. Originally called Mr. Zero, the producers of the 1960's Batman television series called him Mr. Freeze...
—Wikipedia

See Freeze, half-erased by frothing breath,
holding a Golden Age Detective, glove
shivering, as his whisper crystallizes
in the bare air:

> "Zero, you filled a cold spell
> in comic books with cosmic jokes
> against yourself. Your, and I
> quote, *ice crimes* ran like rain."

I have to set him straight: Mr. Freeze,
like an ice cube tray, Zero gave you shape.
That Frigidaire model supersuit
that holds you frozen in human form was his.
That skull-scale snowglobe that holds your head—
blown in the forge where he became vapor.

> "But my story runs out of a more
> killer winter. My wife, my icicle,
> shines in a cryogenic style
> of night, frozen so close to rapture

by cancer." Freeze, forget your style, wife, night.
Soon, your cronies will ride in on their polar bears

to collect sawblades shaped like snowflakes,
to open showcases at the Lifelong
Companion Diamond Exchange,
icing on tonight's heist.

When Batman runs you down there, turn.
Reach for the back of that batmask.
By the cold of your hand flashing past his face,
he'll know he has one. Steal its body heat.
No need to fear it warming you to death.
You're not real.
How does that... feel?

Our Hero *Is* Trapped in the Past!

    Batman, backtrack
past the camp glam of your adolescence,

    to the infantile serials.
There, be deep in slaves of the rising sun

    again. Again, stungun
the Living Corpse that orders them to war.

    Zombie Master Daka
flees the scene, but your bullets Americanize

    them all. War hero,
propaganda's torpedo, your budget was oh so low.

That batsuit—hollow
at the elbows, eyeholes sliding and blinding

    you, too loose, like
a child hid inside. Hero of our country's repressed

    grief, tell me why.
See: I made a bad suit out of infatuation. What

    was just a crush
turned to war against the future. The circuits of her

    nerves turned
to seams from which no treaty could be gleaned.

> Say I'm a slave.
> Say I'm a bad Boy Wonder. Say you'll fly me
>
> > through this black-
> > and-white waking up, you who love nothing
>
> but justice, you
> not shot down with each vanish of a love
>
> > into hovering nothing.
> > Your mourning, in this noir form of you,
>
> > drains its chambers
> at an enemy as obsolete as you need to be.
>
> > It spits out its bullet
> heart, draws Hollywood blood. The End.

The Bat-Can-Can

Orbit our city's new Strobelight District
for a night, and you forget how dark
the sky's gutters[1] are. You find the crowd

blossoming arms and a chrome steam
of pheromones, tossing hair that sweat
and light filter silver, tube tops blooming

and curling to the floor, not Gothamites
Gone Wild, no, the last, sassy fantasies
in the Xanadu you revamped years back

during the numb age of drum & bass. Dazed
by blacklight, stuck to the walls of clubs—
Liquid, Galaxy, places Larry Levis

would have deep-sixed for the Blue Note,
you built this vision: skin, strobelit
so it disappears, or is the only light.

> Batman has his mission here:
> find the Quasivisible Kid, born
> strobing in and out of sight, who
> his parents could see only in intervals,
> who wandered in on the wrong pulse
> of the strobe, perfectly out
> of time, and vanished.

---

[1] Gutters: spaces between comic book frames

Cape wrapped in his fists like a flag
pulled from its pole, mask slack
on his cheeks, Kevlar armor
unraveling, he can-can-can't
keep from dancing, can't keep
his savior nature
in place.

    Fired by cider in a Dublin club, my fiancé
    dissolved and bam evolved
    with her hair a sweaty, lit, melted grid,
    like the city of adulthood we were dancing
    our way into was tousled up
    and growing from her,

    and this kiss she gave me
    like a thick mask was made of her face,
    like her body and mine were two limbs
    the music used, helped me
    feel I didn't need her.

Hands rip at his utility belt.
Shoulders pulse against his chest,
and thump him back.
A thin woman, constellated with silver studs,
yanks at his mask, and he sees
that the catsuit is a tattoo
on her naked body, and he kneels
below the beating hands,
thumbs to his eardrums,
drowning in the crowd.

When we left the dance floor,
let me have seen a single gaslight
standing above the rivers
of kids in their shining skin
and lacquer of clubwear,
where a fire still spiraled,
cycled, into the shape
of a face that cast its mask
against the glass.
Let me not have followed her
to try to disappear in her again.

What clutches at his bent neck
like a spiky ring of twigs,
and what breathes in his ear, "Mister,
I can't see me?" He leans in,
to that vacant-this-second,
thicker-dark-the-next piece of space
and finds that it is crying.

He won't let go.
He'll find the master switch
and shatter it,
and the dancers will find,
like you, that they can
dance, can not disappear, can
move to their own
pulses.

In Honey B

May you, sewn into a bull's hide,
be carried like trash back to your lord.
  —*Ovid, badly translated by me*

We last left our Caped Crusader
cursed with immersion in honey.

If you can't remember him there,
and you suspect this is a meditation
on obsession without empathy,
no.
        It's a post-
        batmanticist poem of lust
        as a sticky mask.

Flash back with me:

        Batman finds his alpha bat wrapped around
        a stalactite. Honey has glazed its wings
        to masking tape. Stalking the sugar mosaic
        it left in his cave, he enters the batacombs.

Sticky-sweet
reader, meet Honey:

        stickiest villainess this side of
        you, a yellow-and-black exoskeleton
        of glitter fits her tight as pollen, and Batman's
        satin skin is buzzing to be touched, and a sting
        combs his heart for a spark of nectar.

Behind her, see the monolithic yellowjacket,
size of an ox, crumpled in the shape
of a bad landing, fuselage of its belly
torn open, blunt shine of a honey mine
inside. Batman goes close to her.

Her tremble-dance caramelizes
the very air. Tears make her cheek SKKK
stick to his.

    Let honey drown the scene.

Flash to an hour after now,
as a honey bee symbol spins
across the screen:

    our hero in a sticky
    dark that he can only know by taste,
    her voice a roil of bubbles
    that break, let their sound out:

Batman, Alexander
the Great died from battering
the world into his mask. His body
was sunk in honey
to keep it looking alive.
I've sealed you in, my poor drone,
to stay this way. Body
too stuck in honey to move,
how will this world not fill your lungs?
Will the writer set you free?

Alexander is my middle name.
He can stay there, that honey bat,
stuck in my place.

    Or you can be near me again.
    Honey, tune in.

Closing Time

Tonight, at last, he'll hang up his mask
for good. It's true. It will sell hella (that's
a lot of) comics. He will make this little hell

freeze over. But first, the underworld has overflowed
again. Batplunger to that can,
he scans the damage.

>
> Clayface, psycho idol made of Play-Doh,
> whose suit holds his body in one, runny piece,
> has lit an abandoned building, to make a kiln,
>   to bake himself back to human again.
>
> Poison Ivy has woven the library in vines,
> sealed the children in their story hour,
> to tell them where
>   their fairy tales really come from.
>
> Twoface has kidnapped the twins
> from the Macy's makeup counter, for a hydrochloric
> makeover. Too late to save them.
>   But wait. There might still be time.
>
> Killer Croc, still in shock from Crocodile
> Hunter Steve leaving us, is running, no,
> more walking amok. But he's too, too
>   close to postal.

They're all here. Call it karmageddon:
if you suit up, they will come. They can't
not. Now, on the city's flowery outskirts,

downed powerlines are ushering the others
in, pencilling their silhouettes with sparks: there's
Scarecrow, here to fear us up. Ras al Ghul;

gulp. Riddler—what's almost as deadly as
needing someone? That's right. It's him.
Hundreds of your Others have come, and Grendel,

because he got lost on the way to becoming
a ghost. They're here; they always were, and are,
to make you stay away from being you.

There's one win here. Turn to me. Talk to me,
like your dad used to to you. Like I still do.
"You're... " No, in caps again, like a comic book's

way of saying, or Bidart, when he stabs at the heart's
dead leather, edge first:

NOW YOU ARE SIX, IN BATMAN JAMJAMS,
PIRATING NIGHTMARES, FIGHTING WITH
YOUR FORGETTING TOMORROW MORNING

THEN, INTO MIDDLE SCHOOL, AND I DIE
MANY TIMES IN THE FIRST ISSUE OF BATMAN
YOU BUY, DIE LIKE YOU WANT TO WANT TO

AND THEN YOU'RE HERE, WATCHING "BATMAN
BEGINS" WITH NO ONE IN YOUR SKIN, NOT
KNOWING HOW YOU'VE BROKEN DOWN.

One day, Batman realized,
when he took off his mask,
the villains turned into children.

>   Tonight, if my nephew runs
>   into the living room, from that heart-dark
>   of his, Batman on his jamjams wearing tears,
>   I'll pick him up, and tell him he's real.

You are, too.
Don't let go

His Valediction Forbidding Becoming Like Him

If you harness, to harvest, hurt
and nurse it into the birth of a persona,

if you love the invisible citizens
nightmares write under my paper,

> pray for the Invisible Scarlet O'Neill
> who fingers a nerve and vanishes,
> who wears the red of bad brides,
> whose black hair is the ex-wife's,
> dipped in ink,
>> you'll sink.
>> Stop. Turn

to the real,
that suit of wounds,
that suit of nudity.

If women still seem to become costumes
to you, if their bodies turn to words
spoken by no one, if they slip
and break you, if their Xray
vision fishes under your skin
and comes up with nothing,

> know you're stuck in my mask.
> Take it off. Ask whatever power

> flutters in your city of a heart
> who you are.

Batellite, Batellite of Love

And you think to yourself what a
wonderful underworld, but Batman's
been turning it into one for so long,
dispensing justice, dependable as Pez,
and no melt of the moment frozen in him,
where his parents die in a storm
he plays eye to, his mask black
and blue, his courage like sugar
transfigured by caramelizing crimes.

So is his grimace like happiness
shrinkwrapped in syntax? Does the volt
of his pulse shock him hot? No. Go
with him out of the alleyways'
shadow mazes, into the moonlight
that inks us mask-blank, look
how it violet-plates the Gotham Bay
waves, wait for the bats to flutter
up carrying narrative accelerant—

a batoscope to hold to sky. At his white
eye, it says what he'd fear, if
he could: aliens have graffitied
the Batellite again. From here,
he sees its riveted wings, its teeth
antennae now spraypainted halo-
gold, but can't make it out. "Up yours,

earthlings," or some patly gangsta
alien slang that will take a freaking day
in inky space with the batsandblaster,

and the fanboys, batpanoptic eyes
shining on this comic book,
pray for it to be a trap, and not
to be a trap, pray that his blue hands
may fail at the rocket fighter's
ignition, a holdover from the camp
1960's, its red echo of art deco
rusted toward blood, pray
as he kicks its engine, say thanks
when it sputters. Starts. Lifts off.

Batman sublimates this planet like
a hidden meaning. The Batellite
calls him, and he lands on its wing,
to feather-dust the droppings of
space mice from their crenelations,
and here, for some dream of a reason,
he can breathe. He can pull in
the coal, six-billion year night, sigh
out all his stresses, kick back
without kicking off into the radii

of asteroids. The graffiti—by the girl
my mind won't quit inking bride-white;
it says *I do, but I don't know that yet,*
and he breathes it in, perfume of a
plotline atomized, or is it the first

fume of morning dew in your nose,
its crystal trickle not like ink
fresh-bloomed on a penciling
of the Joker's acid-blasting flower. No

it's like light on that one field, that
one morning, where you outran
your fear of running fast, that light
on that kind of new-born green
let you forget you were made of lead,
but, batshit, the whole craft is moving
now. Batman motored the batellite
out of its orbit as love distracted me.
He's radioed the coast guard SKK
I'M CRASHLANDING IN THE
BAY. Dolly in like Google Earth,
you'll see Commissioner Gordon
orbiting in cigar-hearted mist. Worlds

are grids. This one is, too. PHOOM
is the sound of him phooming home,
HMM is the sound of the cosmic
optimism he brings with him. Will
the city survive this epiphany? Will
we? Tell me. I'm waiting to write it

Batman Agonistes, or Eyeless in Gotham

Batman's making haiku
in the mask of Samson:
>   *Delilah's wild eyes, /two suns, still set*
>   *in the head,/from which she plucked mine.*

His altar stars a Samson action figure,
eclipsed by his shadow as he chants:
>   *Apostle of muscle, teach me not to stray*
>   *to steroids. Teach me what made you blind idol*
>   *of the Bible. Teach me to live in fame and still*
>   *chase pain of an endless struggle with evil.*

Samson's phantom wafts in, atomized to a mist,
white like the Phantom's eyes in his black mask,
and Milton is a silhouette filtering in behind him
>   as Batman chants *Samson, amen.*
>   And Batman chants, *No, Chad,*
>>   *I'm done chanting. I'm also done idolizing*
>>   *a figurine and playing the batmasochist.*
>>   *These white eyes in my mask*
>>   *aren't negatives of the soul's cave*
>>   *where your inner child is going blind.*

But Batman backtracks,

>   *No, I don't backtrack. I'm Batman.*
>   *My eyes aren't blind; they shine like a bat's,*

> *masked by light. Doesn't that beat*
> *your quest for inner pain to shit?*

Maybe.

> *Okay. Meditate on that in this Batcave.*
> *I'm going out to fight crime. Remember,*
> *I do that. Especially when Vicki Veil*
> *Hey. Spell it right.*
> *Vicki Vale needs a bodyguard*
> *to take her undercover in a bridal shower.*
> *Know what I mean? I'm a superhero,*
> *not the Batmannequin in your picture*
> *window. Finish chasing pain, and go play*
> *outside. Be hypnotized by the eyeshadow*
> *sundown dyes on the skyline,*
> *how the silhouettes of antennae*
> *look like skylashes that wind, not mind,*
> *is batting. But first, sit here and batter*
> *Milton's legacy with your own blank*
> *verse on blindness to God. You want that*
> *so bad.*

Okay. A kid, I prayed, but to the world
to stay away. To me, alone felt whole
and, holy solipsist, my eyes slid closed,
and then the sense of eyelessness began
with I-lessness not far behind. Unseen
because the dream of seeing disappeared,
I turned unreal. The old reality

would merge with my old self outside a mind
that knew it was the only thing alive,
a cave, and I its god. The world appeared
to end my prayer, but as a shattered mirror
I couldn't see me in.
>"*That* was vanity," says
>the phantom of Samson.
>
>"Agony," amends
>Milton's silhouette. Amen.

Bat & Man

*And how bewildered is any womb-born creature
that has to fly. As if terrified and fleeing
from itself, it zigzags through the air, the way
a crack runs through the teacup. So the bat
quivers across the porcelain of evening.*

—Rilke, translated by Stephen Mitchell

Hey, Bruce. Wake up. You're shrieking in your sleep.

Selina. Just a nightmare. Nothing much.
*Not much? Your mumbles kept me up, from bats
to Zorro, then, was someone murdered? That's
my business. But you're drenched in sweat.* Your touch
did that. *Calm down and talk to me.* Too much
to tell. You heard it, anyway. *In bits.
I caught enough to need the rest.* Too late.
It's gone. *Oh, bullshit. Talk. I'll help you. Clutch

me here for inspiration. There.* You purr
like her. *Like who? You're gorgeous. Can't this wait?*
No. *Tell.* But it's a nightmare. *Do your worst.*
You'll learn too much. *I'll live.* This one will haunt
your catnaps. *Spill it. I'm too curious.*
It started by the bay. My parents... spawned.

You dreamed your parents made you by the bay?

When Thomas ramped his roadster up the pier,
its brights electroplated every wave.
His airtight plot: tonight, to put the moves
on Martha Moore, the highest-rated score
at Gotham High. He'd feel away her fear
and work his magic in his favorite cave:
her perfect ear. Not easy, when she shoved
his arm away, and killed his grin with scorn.

He tried a lie: "The bats come here to hunt
at night." *That worked?* She whispered, "Do they bite?"
And night was on his side. A whitewing plunged
across the windshield, clung, its eyes like bits
of living flint. She sprang against him. Tongue
on hers, he blurred her mumbled "but" to "bat."

So bats conceived you, just as much as Tom?

They stayed, and came again, as many nights
as Tom and Martha did. Like living scarves,
they veiled the windshield while my parents loved.
You'd call that love? I dreamed their wedding white.

"I d-d-do," his stutter, fluttered, spat
at Martha's heart. Her muttered echo stirred
the womb they both assumed was bare, no spark
but nerves.
                    But there I germinated, net
of cells and maps of capillary starred
with organs.
                Mother said the wedding march
attracted bats. They charged above the cars
and surged into the crowd, that scattered, lurched,
and scourged them with corsages. Like a scar,
she drew them in. They chased her from the church.

What did you dream then, sobbing in a ball?

That mother knew there was no boy inside
her body. Not so much as human cells
evolved there. Doctors—jokers. Tried to tell
her what was kicking in there was a child.

She felt me—bat. With feather ears, with eyes
like sequins, I would spy. With spindly nails
for fingers, I would scratch for freedom. Sails
of budding wings I fluttered, and she'd die

before she let me out. Hysteria
was Father's diagnosis. All the pills

she took to chase the more material
anxieties away had backfired, built

this womb inside her mind. In tears, he held
her down to sweat it out. Then I went still.

You murmured for your soldiers and your war.

The nursery I was raised in—arsenal,
where suits of armor rusted to their swords
and soldered armies swarmed before their lord,
myself. I crawled along embroidered snarls
of dragons woven into carpets dull
from years of heels. I smelled the antique air
and heard it purr. I felt the paintings glare
above—the ancient Waynes, whose perfect scowls
were turning, as they cracked, into the smiles
of skulls.   At dinner time, a shadow dawned
along my back and drowned the battlefield.
I'd shrink in Mother's shade, her giant hand
a wing I took, that shook, eclipsed and chilled
my own. I loved the Cornish game hens, tan
on silver plates, like hearts on Spartan shields.

You said you made the dark a kinder god.

When Mother's demons came. They bled my dreams
all May. I couldn't sleep, because she screamed
all night. In June, a swarm of nurses came
to take her to "a holiday in Rome".
Then Father's muffled sobs began to chime
away my nights. The nervous servants streamed
upstairs—his cursing at them laced a pain
between my temples.
                        "Come and take me home,"
I prayed. The sky outside my window turned
into the Shadow's coat. The killing moon
became a bullet. Clouds became his guns.
The stars, above their reddish scarf of sunrise,
were his eyes.
                Were masked by bats. "You're mine,"
he hissed in wind. He settled in my skin.

Did heroes guard you through the darkest part?

We went to Gotham Theater to see
"The Mark of Zorro". Tyrone Power wore
the name and cape, eclipsing every score
with gunfire. Such a sweet and distant screen—
I felt the world contract to him and me.
My mother's screams, my father's drunken snore
were shams, or dreams, as blurry as their scars
are now. But then, across the screen, a vein
of darkness ran, like ink, its tip a blade.

Some vandal slashed the screen? Then ran away.
They didn't stop the movie? No, it played,

and Zorro wore a moving wound. *Then?* Stay
in this, a second. Feel the urge to pray

to him? *He's only light, though. So is day.*

You fought your parents just before they died.

With Zorro fliers. Rolled to hollow swords.
We'd fought into an alley. Blind and, worse,
unlit. The dark there muttered, "Lady. Purse."
It grinned. It glittered. Spit-slick, shattered hoards

of teeth. Its pistol bristled holes. He squared
his shoulders. *Tom did?* Yes. Then the dark cursed
and birthed a fire. A roar. Star that ate his shirt
and burst. She howled "You coward." *Mother?* Heard

her lurch. Another fire. And roar.
Star that
                    blazed
so bright, so long, I saw her—mask with ink
exploding
          through its cracks. *The killer?* Spliced
himself into the city night. Erased
     me. *Who did?* Mother. Father. *Shh. Close your eyes*

and think of Arkham. Nightmares took you there?

At night, my father swept across my bed
with batwings, fangs. I'd fly outside; I'd hide
in flight, and wake, somehow, on real grounds
with gargoyles crying rain, that sang, that said

son, son, against my skin. The bats I scared
from cricket-hunting into ivied grids—
the trellises that hid the violent ward
from us, and us from them.
                          I nursed my dread
of death. I cowered on the lawn, saw frost
that furred the tree trunks silver, like the pelts
of all my floating friends. I couldn't trust
this vampire father. *Did he make you crawl
on air, next time, and fall, become a ghost
like him?* I stayed awake. He stayed in hell.

What heroes nursed you in the orphanage?

In Father's leather book of doctor lore—
the bat-masked shaman. Rattles in his wings,
he'd zoom into the spirit world, to bring
the fever-driven patient back to ours.

In Gotham, shaman meant machine—the car,
the cinema, where newsreels lit the flings
of holy criminals who battled gangs,
who went by vigilante. *And they were*

the Shadow? Traveled under every street
with .45s to light his way through hell.

And Phantom? Pantomimed him overseas
on battlefields tiled with Nazi skulls.

And Batman? No. Not him. In violet sheets,
I'd imitate their magic. *Heal by veil?* No. Heal by kill.

You loved the part where partying was life.

The tabloids dubbed the mansion Xanadu,
and you were Kubla Wayne. Yeah. Parties ran
and died just as their orphan sons began,
and bourbon supercharged our hearts. It bloomed

from breasts of marble angels. "Interviewed,
the twenty-something billionaire could stand,
but barely. Tumbler tight in either hand,
he swayed and twirled above the teeming room

where debutantes were dancing, clad in fans.
'A lovely cave,' was all he'd say." A year
I spent in articles I had to scan
to fabricate the night before. It'd disappear
like murder in the drink that ran
from throat to soul, that blurred the crowds to tears.

What made you say the underworld has come?

The Halloween that did me in began
with normal pandemonium. No harm—
a thousand guests in Trojan armor stormed
the decoupage Olympus on the lawn.

I was disguised as Zeus, disguised as swan.

My Leda, blond, anonymous, had come
onstage and doused herself. Some kind of rum
all over her. My memory is gone
of what we'd come there for. The crowd, bronze-stained

with torchlight, chanted, "God" and " Thunder."

        "Zeus,"

she said. My memory grows sharper then:
the bat-calls started. Grew, too loud, too soon.

The crowd began its chant of "God" again
because the bats were blotting out the moon.

Go on.

Above, a flood of silver wings
and branding iron eyes. Below me flowed
the masks of my disintegrating crowd.
They prayed, and strained against the stage. The sting

of smoke and drink had made me blind. I think
the bats attacked, and some caught fire. A cloud
of smoke careened up to me, keening. Now,
I know I should have fought it. Then, I sank

to Leda, where she screamed, her hair a net.
The burning bat flew into it. The more
she fought, the tighter it was caught. It lit

her scalp. *You put it out?* I tried. The more
I tried... *There there.* The more the fire caught
and spread. She sputtered "Why," my dying star.

*This really happened. I remember. You went
underground.*

No resurrection came. Just cops. My name
got rid of them. I hid. I shut the blinds
in every room then, fired light and time
and all my other servants. Not alone

enough, I stumbled through the gloom, a gleam
of family memory lit my way. My mind
retreated, left the dark an open seam
I fell into. Inside my chest, a stone

was growing. Maybe weeks, I drank. The dark
and bourbon drowned the scene. *Until your fall.*
I woke, face-down, below the basement stairs,
my chest and throat a red brocade. The scald
and cold—I'd crushed my tumbler. Crystal shards—
here are the scars. *They're shallow.* But they glowed.

Some nightmare fire erupted from your wounds?

No phosphorous or poltergeist, just cuts
with constellating glass, that cast a light
to split the limestone gloom below to slats
and jamb. I'd found a door. It couldn't, must
be Father's cellar door. Lit up. *With what?*
An orange glow was pulsing from inside.
I had to break it. *Bad bat.* "Sorry, Dad,"
I prayed, and kicked the frame. Again. It burst,

exhaled a veil of smoke. Behind it, floor—
but no. The dream gets weirder here. *Why? Where*
I set my feet was just a shaft of air
descending to a monolithic pyre
how many hundred feet below. It snared
me. *Then I woke you back into the here*

and now. Some dream—sounds Batmanic to me.

You're borrowing from him. Selina, don't
say that... It's true. Your voice was even toned,
as low as his when you talked it through. You know
his life and voice? Know why I'm always out

at night? Don't tell me—you become a cat.
Ha ha. Really— Don't tell me. It's too soon
for me to see another side of you.
Just stay my... my night sky. You're no poet.

You're just a boy. I'm more than that. You're Bat—
I'm what? Oh, bad, I said. Okay. Hey. Lie
here next to me some more, and we'll forget
that nightmare life you've spun for me. I'd like
that, but I can't. That sound, under the bed?
My phone. I... have to go. Then so do I.
                              Goodnight. Good bat.

Batman Leaves a Sonnet On Catwoman's Voicemail

Your whip was at the crime scene. Break-in, there
at Gotham's Petting Zoo. Cat burglary—
you took a cage of lynxes. Dawned on me
to search the floor for fur, and I found hair

too long and straight, too dark, just like your stare;
been searching zoos, invading surgeries
in animal hospitals all night; I need
you to get back to me, Selina. I swear

your alter ego's name is safe with me.
I need it that way, need her to stay clear
and skylined on the skyscrapers, to flee

from me, but not this far ahead. I'm near
now, on the fire escape. Pick up. I see
your shadow on the blinds. I hear your purr.

Acknowledgements

The Batcave *Carbon Copy*, Spring 2012
Notes for the Comic Book Artist to See By (as "Notes for a Comic Book") *Another Chicago Magazine* 48
Opening Night (as "Batman's Opening Night") *Carbon Copy*, Spring 2012
Batman In Honey *Hotel Amerika*, winner of the 2005 poetry contest, reprinted in the *Drawn to Marvel* anthology
Is Batman Trapped in the Past? *Quarterly West*, Spring/Summer 2006
Osiris *hilobrow*
Batplaning Over the Rainbow (as "Batman Over the Rainbow") *The Pinch* 26.1
In Mr. Freeze's Glacierworks *hilobrow*
Our Hero is Trapped in the Past! (as "Batman is Trapped in the Past!") *Quarterly West*, Spring/Summer 2006
In Honey B (as "Batman in Honey B") *Another Chicago Magazine* 48
Closing Time *hilobrow*
Batellite, Batellite of Love *Black Warrior Review* Spring/Summer 2008, winner of the Third Ever Poetry Contest, included in the *Drawn to Marvel* anthology
So bats conceived you, just as much as Tom?, You murmured for your soldiers and your war (as "You must have learned of heroes before words"), Did all your heroes come out of the dark?, and What heroes nursed you in the orphanage? *Diagram* 5.6, included in the *Drawn to Marvel* anthology
Batman Leaves a Sonnet on Catwoman's Voicemail *hilobrow*

A version of the "Bat & Man" sonnet sequence was published as an illustrated chapbook, *Bat & Man: A Sonnet Comic Book*, by Finishing Line Press (illustrated by Mark Cudd).

About the author

Chad Parmenter's poems have appeared in *Best American Poetry*, *AGNI*, *Kenyon Review*, and *Plume*. His chapbook, *Weston's Unsent Letters to Modotti*, won Tupelo's 2013 Snowbound Chapbook Contest. His prose about poetry has appeared in *American Poetry Review* and *Voltage*. Two of his plays, *The Short Knight* and *The Rat Trap*, were included in the Comedies in Concert series at the University of Missouri, where he received his PhD.

www.ingramcontent.com/pod-product-compliance
Lightning Source LLC
Chambersburg PA
CBHW022021290426
44109CB00015B/1256